The Four Day Creative Brief

The Four Day Creative Brief

A Practical Guide for Writing an Inspiring One

Yadira Santana-Dowling

Yadira Santana-Dowling
Copyright 2020
Inspira Communications, LLC
Miramar, Florida

All rights reserved.

This book or any portion thereof may not be reproduced or used in any manner whatsoever without the express written permission of the author except for the use of brief quotations in a book review.

20 21 22 23 LSC 10 9 8 7 6 5 4 3 2 1

Table of Contents

Dedication	1
Chapter 1 - Intro & Three Fundamental Beliefs	3
Chapter 2 - Day One, Discovery	7
Chapter 3 - Day Two, Discovery Part II	11
Chapter 4 - Day Three, Write First Draft	17
Chapter 5 - Day Four, Revisit & Share your Creative Brief	27
Chapter 6 - The Briefing Experience	29
Additional Resources	31

Dedication

This book is dedicated to the tapestry of people whose shoulders I stand on and continue to support me:

Mami, Papi, my love Elvin, my siblings, nieces, nephews and my raison de vivre: Josiah, Joshua and Jahnissi. If not for the work ethic, dedication and love I've learned from you, this book would not be a reality.

To all the teachers, professors, coaches and trainers that have poured their knowledge and love into the person and professional I've become, I am because you are.

To all the amazing coworkers I've had throughout this journey, many of whom I'm fortunate to call friends, I am thankful that the universe thought it fit to cross our paths. I appreciate your continuous support, your patience as I picked your brain or took you though my special briefing experiences and above all, for all the shared laughs.

Thank you!

Chapter 1 - Intro & Three Fundamental Beliefs

Welcome to my brief writing journey, I'm glad you picked up this book and I hope in the end you are more the wiser.

First, let me introduce myself. I've been working in the ad industry as a strategist since summer of 2003 when I had my first internship through the Multicultural Advertising Intern Program, affectionately known as MAIP. After graduating with a Master's degree in Strategy from the VCU Brandcenter in 2004, I moved back home to NYC. Since, I've worked at four different agencies, in New York and Miami, which have contributed useful building blocks for the process I share with you throughout this book. What I share here is what I've learned over the years through my collective work experience along with my unique personal touches that I believe has made the brief writing process more efficient and enjoyable for all involved, hence *The Four Day Creative Brief*.

Before you delve into the book, I'd like to share the foundation of my particular process, what I call The Three Fundamental Beliefs. If we don't agree on these, friend, then no need to read any further because these beliefs are the foundation for every other word in this book.

There are three fundamental beliefs I have that have colored my approach to work. In the following pages, I outline these beliefs because they'll help you understand the rest of the book.

The First is Veracity

The work that we do needs to be founded on truth. Consumers are already skeptical about our work, so if we want to be effective, we need to ground our work in truth. Remember that nobody likes to be sold to, but everyone loves to buy.

When I graduated from VCU Brandcenter with a Master's degree in Strategic Planning, I themed my portfolio "Veracity" because I felt it captured my overall approach, but most importantly, it captured the reason why I went into the industry in the first place.

I decided to become a strategist because I knew of a truth that I felt no one was talking about - a boom of Bicultural Americans were coming of age in the United States as we entered the 20th century. I could foresee that the tapestry of America was changing because there were many people like my siblings, my friends and I who were graduating with college degrees and entering the workforce, yet, there were no major networks or advertisers speaking directly to us. We were part of that "Latino Boom," that was entering a life stage where we would have significant disposable income, which presented an opportunity that many would want to seize. Entering this life stage along with the many positions I held in student government back in High School led me to think: "I can be that voice. I can be the one to provide insight into our minds and hearts that will forever dance in between two cultures without ever feeling like we have to compromise." All because playing this role was not new to me, I had enjoyed being this voice in different capacities all along.

By walking in MY truth, I could shorten the distance between the proverbial *them* and *us* like I had done many times before.

The Second is Creativity Starts with How the Assignment is Presented

I am a super fan of the creative process and at the same time I like to think I know my role as a strategist and not overstep as a copywriter or art director. Because I'm such a fan of creativity, I infuse it into the work that I do as well and how I present the assignment to creatives. This has been my trademark, one that I've found most enjoyable as well.

As a child I would always lean into creative endeavors, I made my own toys out of telephone wire, knit their clothes and made their houses out of cardboard. I spent hours playing and flexing my creative muscles and the time always seemed short because I was having fun. As an adult, I chose a career in advertising because I thought it was the most creative part of any business and it was a legitimate career. It didn't require business attire and pantyhose (I hated wearing those in my finance days - probably the two longest years of my life). Advertising was, and is, for me the industry where I can show up exactly as I am, with my passions and quirks, and be welcome as a productive team member.

I figured if I have this incessant need to create, I must find a way to infuse it into my day to day, because *"if you love what you do, you never work a day in your life"*. I figured out ways to do the daily work of brief writing and presentations by mixing the brainy, research and truth loving with the playful, funny, play-doh and crayon loving sides of me. This is how my right and left brain dance daily.

This is why I've embraced the idea that creativity doesn't start with the creative department, as many would believe, creativity starts with how the assignment is delivered and that's a planner/strategist's job. Planners and strategists have creative licenses too, if you didn't know, now you know. Own it!

The Third and final truth is Adults want to Play Too

One of my greatest discoveries in the past 16 years is that we all have a child inside of us and we bring him/her to work every day. Regardless of how well-behaved or irreverent we are, we want to play too.

Experience taught me this.

I remember working on a project while I was working on my master's, it was for a launch of the laundry line for a well-known brand. My class was tasked with doing research to inform consumer behavior in the category. Part of our research approach entailed sending a packet to moms around the country asking them to complete collages and answer questions about their laundry process. One mom's packet in particular has stayed with me throughout the years because she rubbed a dryer sheet on the papers in her packet so when we opened it upon receipt, her work smelled like a laundry room, instantly placing us all THERE!

This mom's approach captivated us because it was unexpected, engaging more of our senses and thereby our ability to process the information in more ways than we could've imagined at the onset of the assignment. This experience taught me that there's more we can pull from one another by engaging all of our creative selves.

Serge Bloch said it best *"Creativity is the art of combining a little idea with another little idea, you may have another little idea, and so on...at the end maybe a great idea will come up."*

When we capture someone using our creativity, the exchange in return is a richer capture of their intellect.

If you are still tracking along, turn the page to embark on the four day journey I follow to write an inspiring creative brief.

Chapter 2 - Day One, Discovery

Discovery has two phases, essentially breaking down a four Cs situational analysis into two different days of focus.

Starting with the first C: *The Client*

- Let's start from the beginning, making it from scratch means you know nothing about the client nor the industry they are part of so there are questions we need to answer here. This is often the case when dealing with new business pitches.

A client may sometimes provide a lot of useful internal information but sometimes they may not have or may not be able to share said information. This is where we start our digging. If you're provided a client brief, congratulations, you're ahead of the game. If you are not, start your digging by using secondary sources - data that is available to the public, Google, Google Scholar, Hoovers, social media, their website, etc.

What you are looking to answer in the client portion of this section are the following questions:

- Positioning in the marketplace. What is the message they're putting out there about themselves to entice the consumer? Are they using a tagline? This is typically where brands pack their differentiating factor.
- What are the most appealing products and services the client provides to a consumer?
- What are the client's best and worst selling products or services?
- Is the company in good standing? Any press we need to be aware of as we plan their marketing effort?

- Who are the stakeholders that will have a say in the development of this effort?
- What does the client do better than anyone else in the category? What's the competitive advantage?

Finally, what is the history or background of this client? Are they brand new to the market? Are they established with a long history in the market or community?

Moving on to the second C: *The Competition*

After you have gained enough understanding of the client and their business, it is time to look at everyone else that plays in a similar space. These may be direct competitors - companies that sell a similar product or service, or indirect competitors - companies that may offer an alternative product or service. For example, a garden's direct competitor is another garden, whereas their indirect competitor is a museum, both offering a nice visit and a couple of hours of entertainment.

When researching the competitors, here's what I like to answer:

Start by identifying the top direct competitors and the top indirect competitors.

For each competitor, I seek:

- Similarly to the client, positioning in the marketplace. What is the message they have been putting out there about themselves to entice the consumer? Are they using a tagline? This is typically where brands pack their differentiating factor.
- Look and feel. What are their brand colors? What does their logo look like? Do they have a modern or dated image?
- What are their strengths and weaknesses in comparison to our client?
- What target are they going after or speaking to?

- What is their ranking in the industry? Are they the leader? #2 trying harder? Or lost in categorical noise?
- Samples of their communication in as many mediums available as possible: TV ad, radio ad, online ads, social media, web page.

Chapter 3 - Day Two, Discovery Part II

Now onto the third C: *The Consumer*

This the section that creatives look to Planners and Strategists for their expertise, this is the crux of the Strategic Planning discipline - we are the experts in consumer behavior. Malcom Gladwell, in his book Outliers, concluded that one needs 10,000 hours of dedication to a particular discipline in order to be considered an expert. Now, realistically speaking, we know most projects will not afford us the opportunity to spend 10,000 hours studying a singular target, this will take over a year and very little sleep. However, we can apply strategy to how we research and study our subject.

First, the most obvious starting point is demographics. Is there a gender, age, family composition or geography of the folks we need to be targeting? If so, what would those be? Has the client provided this and if so, do we agree with the delineations the client provided?

Next, psychographic targeting, what some may understand as behavioral targeting. This is when demographics do not matter as much as people's mindset, beliefs, essentially their psychological approach to the category. For example, if I'm a hardware store doing a springtime gardening effort, I don't care about the age of the gardener, I rather reach people that will be spending time gardening, that care about plants and growing their own fruits and veggies - this might be a millennial that's into the Farm to Table trend or a retired grandma that likes to line her entry way with Tulips and perennials.

As we embark on the path to discovery of who these people are and how they behave in the category, our goal is to find a differentiating insight that can serve as the first cornerstone of the advertising campaign.

As we search for this 'insight' I find the need to define it, since in my experience it is one of the most misused words in an agency's vocabulary. The dictionary definition of an insight is *a deep understanding of a person or thing*. I want to push it to include the interpreter's intuition and judgement of the data s/he has discovered.

Spewing data in the target section falls short of the job, merely pointing at the behavior of the target also falls short. We need to interpret the behavior and data discovered to come up with an observation that takes a leap beyond what the average person would come up with, because at the end of the day, you want to be the most unique and creative and this is where uniqueness gets its DNA.

As you complete this section, ask yourself these questions: What is it that I see that someone else may not see? What is it about the target's life that makes this offering interesting and relevant? Why should people care about the brand's offering? Lastly, have I gone beyond the data in how I've captured and described the target audience?

Word of advice, get creative in your information gathering. There are industry standard tools that you can use to get at the "why" of peoples' behaviors, I've listed some that I find very effective at the end of the book. In addition, take some time to go observe the consumer in their element, go to a grocery store or department store and walk around, to notice what people are looking at, how they shop, don't be afraid to spark up a conversation about the type of product you're researching. People generally like sharing their opinions to someone that genuinely wants to hear them. Nowadays it is much easier and cost-effective to poll and survey people, come up with provoking questions to help you understand peoples' "why."

Example: Once I had an assignment to research women's behavior around foot care and in my research I noticed that women were creatively personalizing this particular brand's shoes. This led me to connect that women wanted to have comfort but not sacrifice style and were specifically going the extra mile to decorate. I saw this behavior as an opportunity for the brand to add pattern to their insole product as a complement to the dangling of shoes that many women do, this way they would not be embarrassed by the look but rather see it as an exciting reveal of their personalities. This series of extrapolations are what I consider as insights, studying the behavior and jumping into a conclusion that crystalizes a future opportunity for the brand.

Here's a simple example of what an insightful target statement is and what it isn't:

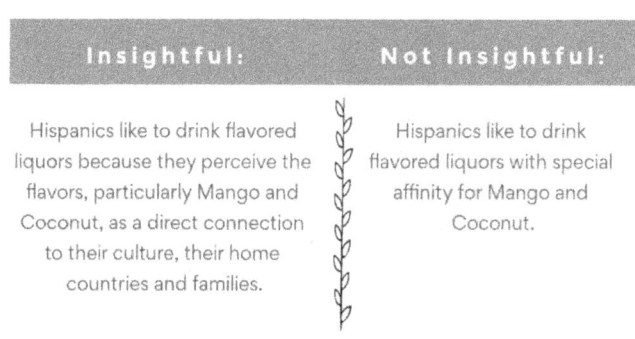

Insightful:	Not Insightful:
Hispanics like to drink flavored liquors because they perceive the flavors, particularly Mango and Coconut, as a direct connection to their culture, their home countries and families.	Hispanics like to drink flavored liquors with special affinity for Mango and Coconut.

Tip: *If you struggle to find nuggets that lead you to insightful revelations, change your research approach to one that is more creative, this unlocks and gives you access to parts of the consumers' brain that you may not be exposed to otherwise.*

Here are some of the questions I seek to answer when doing this research:

- Who seems to be the ideal target? Push beyond demographics.
- Is there a difference between who is currently buying the products or services and who the ideal target should be?
- How do they feel about the category? How do they feel about my client's brand and particular product or service?

- What are the greatest motivators to purchase?
- What does the consumer want when buying in this space? **More often than not, it's not just the product or service but the emotional payoff of having said product or service.**

Now onto the fourth and final C: *The Culture*

This is the most forgotten and underestimated part of a situation analysis. Most would stop at the third C but you my friend, will think through this fourth one as well because you're awesome like that!

The Culture, plain and simple, refers to what is going in our culture - the collective world we live in, the societal landscape in terms of people's attitudes and behaviors. This is one of those areas that impact human beings on a daily basis, yet we hardly talk about this piece of the puzzle that impacts the way we think.

The easiest example of culture to grasp nowadays is the political climate, it impacts us on a daily basis. Some may refrain from talking about it and some are extra vocal, both are manifestations of the impact it has on all of us. Now what does this have to do with advertising, you may ask? Quite a bit! Many people make their purchase decisions based on their perception of the company that is providing the goods and services. If the company is perceived to be on a different side of the aisle from where the consumer is, that company may lose that sale. I can attest that I've stopped using a very convenient service because of this particular reason. Many consumers are savvy enough to realize how they choose to spend their dollars is a powerful statement in and of itself, therefore they exercise the right to vote with it.

Some additional examples of culture driving how consumers interact with brands is the increased concern for planet earth and our environment. Many consumers are now weighing environmental impact as they make buying decisions, this is manifesting in everything from the choice of a convenience store that uses bags that don't contribute to plastic pollution, or the choice to purchase water based on the container it comes in, to the kinds of cars they're choosing to drive, hello Tesla!

As you research societal trends, you want to figure out how people think or feel, and what kind of things are important to them. The questions I seek to answer with this research are as follows:

- Are there any collective opinions that have become popular or unpopular?
- Are there any economic or cultural trends that may impact consumers purchasing habits in this particular industry?
- Are there new technologies or trends that are changing the way people consume in this space?
- Are there any new governmental regulations that impact my client's business and how is my client addressing these?

Chapter 4 - Day Three, Write First Draft

By now, if you have followed the research guide in the last two chapters, you have a wealth of information to use when writing your brief. I have seen plenty of brief templates, I've even been tasked with developing new ones a couple of times through my career. It is important to know that every agency has their own version and in this chapter I'll outline the ones I think are crucial to writing a brief that is packed with insightful information yet concise, clear and to the point.

In addition, I've provided little nuggets of research along the way so that you may have direct insight into your target, your internal clients - the creatives. In order to build this section, I ran a survey asking in-house and agency creatives for their opinions of the brief and briefing process to help you understand the impact our work has on their work.

The sections I recommend are as follows:

- **Background**
- **Objective**
- **Target**
- **SMPI (single most persuasive idea) or USP (unique selling proposition)**
- **RTBs (Reasons To Believe)**
- **Mandatories & Deliverables**
- **KPIs (Key Performance Indicators)**

Remember the key here is to write a brief that is *brief*!

Background

The background section answers the question of Why are we making this effort?

A good creative brief starts with background information that corresponds to the client's motivation for spending money on marketing. The first wave of information is typically provided by the client:

- What is the business problem we are trying to solve?
- What business priority will this effort help to drive or to deliver?
- Do they have a marketing strategy? If so, what is it?
- Are there any specific marketing goals that have been set and we need to achieve? For example: Increase awareness? Increase market share? Increase sales by x%?
- What have I learned about the competition? How has this information colored the landscape we will be working in?

In this section, you want to enter anything we need to understand about the landscape - competitive landscape, business landscape, internal landscape in terms of the company in order to write a creative brief.

This section doesn't need to be long. It can be a couple of sentences summarizing this type of information, keep it straightforward and concise, no embellishment needed.

Objective

This section should outline the overall objective of the effort and it should be a single thing that we are trying to do that ladders back up to the marketing objective, or the company's priorities for the year.

This may be to sell 100 units of a vehicle or to increase sales by X percent.

This is a very important step that helps avoid major issues later on, so it is imperative to keep this part focused. If you're trying to do too much with a singular effort, the effort will turn out ineffective because different strategies are needed if you are trying to build upon where a brand is than if you're trying to rebrand a company or trying to sell a particular product.

It is also important for all involved parties to agree on the objective early on, everyone involved should be on the same page about what the effort needs to *do*. This section is in direct correlation to how the effort's performance will be measured, which is another reason it is imperative that all involved parties agree on the objective before the creative process starts.

Target

This is one of my favorite sections, because this is where we, planners and strategists, get to flex our muscles and demonstrate research, writing and poetic skills. Another reason I love this section is because I think of the target as my friends, it is my job to know them well enough to be able to speak for them. They're not in the room I'm in so this is where I get to be their mouthpiece and I work hard to get it right. I once joked around with a client and told him I had the consumer on 'speed dial' because we had done so much research and work together that I felt like these were *my peeps!*

Start by culling the information you obtained when researching the consumer. What are the 3-5 key things you found most interesting, unique and relevant making them worthy of occupying this space on your brief? Is there something you observed or discovered that led you to make a "judgement call" on their behavior or interests that they didn't exactly express? This is insight.

FACTS:

70% of creatives say a target description that goes beyond demographics is a necessary component of a successful briefing.

In this section, make sure you answer: Who are we trying to connect with? This should include demographics and psychographics. Then push yourself to extract insights. Ask yourself: Am I sharing something here that can offer an "aha" moment for my creative audience? Last but not least, address the shift. Some brief versions include the mind shift that is needed in its own section, I prefer to address that in this section. It is essentially knowing what the consumer reality is, what they're thinking, feeling and behaving like vs. what we want them to think, feel and behave like.

Keep this section focused, you've learned a LOT but you don't have to include all of it, just the most relevant findings. Write it in a way that is cohesive, connected, makes sense and is pleasant to read, this is where you get to channel your poetic side.

After you complete this section, go back and reread it, is there a more creative way of expressing the key things you're trying to communicate about your target? Now that you have the most relevant meat on paper, flex your creative muscle as you rewrite the content.

FACTS:

83% of creatives wish creative briefs were more insightful, providing unique information about the target.

SMPI

"Creators manipulate and reconfigure existing ideas and forms."

This is my other most favorite section. How can I have two more favorite sections you ask? Well, one is a close second!

This is perhaps the section that generates the most thought and also the section that generates the most controversy once shared. Staring at the cursor before you write it can be paralyzing because soooo much hinges on this one statement.

This statement goes by many names - the Single Most Persuasive Idea or the Unique Selling Proposition. Whatever you call it, it is the most important message you need to tell a potential consumer that would persuade them to buy the widget. It is not the *messages*, it is THE message. It is not what the agency wants to say, it is not what the client wants to say, it is what the CONSUMER needs to hear in order to buy. Single minded is important because it's intended to be an elevator pitch that many consumers [that don't spend their whole day thinking about the product] will have to get in just 15 seconds. What is the ONE greatest thing you can tell them? Why should consumers care?

When writing this statement, the following research should be dancing around in your mind: The unique void and fertile ground you discovered when researching the competition, what the consumer is looking for in this space, what are they thinking? What are their beliefs? What do they yearn for? And lastly but definitely not least, how can the widget out deliver the competition and the consumer yearning?

When you come up with a statement, write it down, your first one may not be the most elegant and might be too long but that's okay, it's a start. You then go ahead and deconstruct your first statement and come up with different ways to deliver the same message. Here's where I grant you creative license, have fun with it - is there a catchy way of saying it? Is there a shorter way of saying it? Is there a quote you know that gets at this message? Is there a punchline that can deliver this message? Don't be shy, this is where you get the edge, this is where the widget becomes the lady in red dancing in a room full of grays.

Here are two pieces of advice that I practice, number one is walking away after I've written a couple of versions of the SMPI. I typically do this the day before the brief is due so that I have plenty of thinking time and subconscious time to sit with the idea. I like to revisit it on my drive home and my drive back to work because I can come up with more creative ways to express it after I've let my brain do a couple of laps. The number two thing that I like to do is share it with others, particularly with creatives for their opinion on which version is the most inspiring to the ultimate user of the statement - themselves. This practice was required at one of the agencies I worked in and it was brilliant, worked so well I took it as a rule for myself. Unfortunately this is not the norm but I advise it because the whole briefing process goes so much smoother. Think about it, they have the chance to ask questions and you get to answer them and clarify your work before you're in a room full of people looking for your direction.

The last part that begs clarification before we leave this section is communication strategy vs. business strategy. First, let us deconstruct and start with strategy, it is by definition a plan of action. The confusion stems from the business vs. the communication part. Business strategy is what the client provides or if you're a business consultant, this is what you recommend they do, develop the plan of action for the business. It may be something like this: I have a business and I have a 5 product portfolio, for Q4 I want to sell product #3 because it provides my greatest profit margin and it's the most relevant during that time of the year. All efforts should be focused on product #3, let's sell a bunch of product #3!!!!! That my friend, is business strategy.

Now, communication strategy goes back to the SMPI or USP, what is the communication plan? This is what you communicate to the masses to persuade them to buy product #3. This may be written like this:

Celebrate the warmest and fuzziest of holidays with product #3.

For Nike, it might be something like this:

Nike empowers the athlete in all of us.

For Volvo, it might be something like this:

For those with precious cargo, there's Volvo.

This is where the money is as a creative thinker, persuasion is part art, go flex your creative muscles and come up with an exciting and motivating proposition!

FACTS:

70% of creatives agree the most valuable take away from a creative brief is campaign inspiration.

Reasons to Believe (aka RTBs)

"The consumer is not a moron, she's your wife. You insult her intelligence if you assume that a mere slogan and a few vapid adjectives will persuade her to buy anything." - David Ogilvy

This section holds the proof of the pudding you're working hard to make. This is not a laundry list of every single thing that can be possibly said about the product or service. Rather, it is a list of a few curated facts, benefits or usability details that support the message you're delivering in your SMPI.

Beware of including too many things in this section because this section can lead you astray and fragment your main message. Keep it focused, and exclude anything that doesn't work as a proof point.

If you run into a client that wants to include everything about their product in this section before they approve your brief (it happens), ask them to prioritize and remind them that a campaign as a whole can deliver many messages but one single piece may only be able to deliver the most important ones. Different mediums lend themselves to different levels of messaging.

Lastly, remember to keep it truthful, no fluff. The *truth* shall set you free!

Mandatories & Deliverables

This section is pretty self-explanatory, these are direct instructions for what the creative department needs to deliver.

The first thing we tackle are mandatories provided by clients. Is this a promotional effort that requires a specific logo lock up or offer? Does it correspond to a special anniversary or milestone? The clients may have already developed graphics and these need to be provided to the creatives for them to include. Are there key points or legal disclaimers that need to be included when advertising this product or service? All of these details go here.

The next portion is the deliverables. This may be a list of specs or types of ads that need to be developed as part of this campaign or effort. This section is highly dependent on where you are in the creative process, if the team is developing a brand new campaign, the deliverables might be three unique concepts before getting into the specifics of what is on the media plan. If the media has been planned and what is needed in terms of output has already been outlined, then get your list of deliverables from there. Ask for support in answering this question from the media team if your agency has one or from the account team.

Key Performance Indicators (aka KPIs)

The second to last portion of your brief should outline the key performance indicators. The content for this section comes from your discovery and you've got hints of it in your objectives. This is an agreement among all parties involved on how the success of the effort will be measured. This is imperative because you take pride in your work (*I know because you're reading this book*) and want to avoid a client that says "the campaign didn't work." Have some wisdom, learn from my mistakes, I have regretted the one time I recall not including this detail early on.

So with that said, how will you know the work has been successful? Are they looking for sales? Everyone is, and it is valid to include. Consider all consumer touch points and include measures here. Some media will be measured by impressions, engagements, click through rates (CTRs) or video completion rates (VCRs). Some others will be measured by phone calls made to vanity numbers to track which ad reached that particular consumer. Consider all touch points and develop your list, share with internal teams and clients to ensure all stakeholders are on the same page.

Trust me on this, you'll be glad you did!

Timeline

This last section is self-explanatory and you must have it. It is provided by the project manager or traffic department. This lets your team know what they have to do by when.

Projects run so smoothly when they're organized from the start. The most pleasant work experiences I've had have one thing in common, strong project managers.

Chapter 5 - Day Four, Revisit & Share your Creative Brief

By now my friend, you've written the first draft of your brief. Congratulations! I trust you've reread it a few times to catch any errors and to ensure the thoughts are as you intended them and are easily understood.

Here's something I know for sure, every brief can benefit from at least one additional set of eyes.

I worked at an agency that had a peculiar process that I ended up falling in love with and that was sharing the brief with creatives first before anyone else could see it. This allowed for clarity checking and answering questions before we got to the briefing table. It also confirmed the brief's main focus was indeed inspiring to its intended audience. Sometimes I would have various propositions or directions I could take the campaign in and I would bring the various angles to this meeting and collaborate on narrowing down to the most fruitful and differentiating ones. The very first time I tried this process I was nervous, but since then I noticed this process pursued the most perfect collaboration between creatives and planners. The benefits became so obvious to me that now it's my preferred modus operandi.

After sharing with creatives, I share with coworkers that are also invested in this effort, they might be account managers, social strategists or management. My approach is always collaborative, listening to everyone's perspectives and having healthy discussions on what content would get us the best outcome. I am not possessive and I am not rigid, if I disagree with anyone's perspective I explain why. There's usually something I've discovered in research that others may not be privy to that I can point to for my disagreement. I love letting data tell the story because we can operate with a greater degree of confidence.

Last but not least, I share with clients. Similarly to my approach with internal stakeholders, I share the brief with clients and give them the opportunity to ask questions and suggest any adjustments before approving the brief. Some clients will require more additional work than others. Some clients are not in the habit of approving the first version of the brief. Give it time, learn their patterns, engage in healthy discussions and above all remember that you guys share the same goal.

After you have received all feedback, address it. If the changes are significant, ones that alter the direction of the brief, go back through the sharing process again and of course, ask to adjust the timeline if you need to. If the changes are not drastic, go ahead and proceed to the last part, the briefing experience.

Remember exercise builds muscle, at first you might feel out of your comfort zone through this process but the more you practice it the more natural you'll be following it.

Chapter 6 - The Briefing Experience

I would dare to say that the briefing experience is taken for granted by most and in my estimation, it provides the greatest opportunity for the exchange of creative spark. Think of all the work and creativity that has brought the brief this far and now you, my planner friend, get to deliver it to the folks that will use it to create magic. Since magic is what is expected, you must make this exchange experience magical.

The part of the briefing experience that I deem most important is first deciding in your mind that it will be fun. If you're having fun, chances are you can transfer that attitude and energy to a full room.

Next, get into the creative psyche as you prepare. Anticipate their questions, ponder on what you think will get them excited and inspired.

"All creators, even the most celebrated ones, draw on the work of others, influenced consciously or not by what's come before - and what's happening around them." - Anthony Brandt and David Eagleman

It is a planner's job to give creatives a spring board. Help them have fun. I discovered that no matter the age, everyone wants to have fun. I have brought crayons, pipe cleaners and play-doh to rooms full of clients and all kinds of agency folks and everyone has welcomed the activities as a breath of fresh air. Be the fun that you want your work to be, be the fun that you want to have in a one-hour meeting. If it is to be, it's up to you!

Last but not least, make sure there's a clear link between your activities and the strategy you want to deliver. This is what you need to think about and prepare for, the brief has already been written, now you get to turn it 5x over in your head to find the most creative way to deliver the SMPI. In my experience, I have facilitated product testing when we needed to advertise new launches; I once did tabletop bonfire and s'mores when the SMPI had something to do with fire; and I've had teams cook something as a group to have them grasp the concept of food in the Hispanic family.

> **FACTS:**
>
> 88% of creatives agree briefing experiences effectively jumpstarted their creative thoughts.

I have pulled from my interests because they compose the arsenal of my experiences. You my friend, pull from all of your interests to create something beautifully unique. This is why you may have heard that the most interesting employees are not workaholics but those that have a life outside of the agency, because they bring those life experiences to make a richer agency table.

And after you've done all you can, have fun!

Additional Resources

Here are a list of tools I use and highly recommend to assist in your life as a strategist.

Secondary Research: mintel.com, www.trends.google.com

Syndicated Research: oneview.simmonsresearch.com

Word Clouds: wordclouds.com

Target persona template: Xtensio.com

Four Cs Situational Analysis:

https://www.volusion.com/blog/situation-analysis-the-5-cs/

Books:

The Art of the Pitch by Peter Coughter

The Hero and The Outlaw by Margaret Mark

Let's connect:

Facebook: https://www.facebook.com/Inspiracom/

LinkedIn:

https://www.linkedin.com/in/yadira-santana-dowling-07b7673/

www.inspiracommunications.com

CPSIA information can be obtained
at www.ICGtesting.com
Printed in the USA
LVHW091307140520
655612LV00003B/32/J